merry Christmas!!

love,
Denise

TRUTHFORLIFE®

THE BIBLE-TEACHING MINISTRY OF **ALISTAIR BEGG**

The mission of Truth For Life is to teach the Bible with clarity and relevance so that unbelievers will be converted, believers will be established, and local churches will be strengthened.

Daily Program

Each day, Truth For Life distributes the Bible teaching of Alistair Begg across the U.S., and in several locations outside of the U.S. on over 1,700 radio outlets. To find a radio station near you, visit *truthforlife.org/station-finder.*

Free Teaching

The daily program, and Truth For Life's entire teaching archive of over 2,000 Bible-teaching messages, can be accessed for free online and through Truth For Life's full-feature mobile app. A daily app is also available that provides direct access to the daily message and daily devotional. Download the free mobile apps at *truthforlife.org/app* and listen free online at *truthforlife.org.*

At-Cost Resources

Books and full-length teaching from Alistair Begg on CD, DVD and MP3CD are available for purchase *at cost, with no mark up*. Visit *truthforlife.org/store.*

Where To Begin?

If you're new to Truth For Life and would like to know where to begin listening and learning, find starting point suggestions at *truthforlife.org/firststep.* For a full list of ways to connect with Truth For Life, visit *truthforlife.org/subscribe.*

Contact Truth For Life

P.O. Box 398000 Cleveland, Ohio 44139
phone 1 (888) 588-7884   **email** letters@truthforlife.org
 /truthforlife   @truthforlife   truthforlife.org

Alistair Begg

Christmas

Playlist

Four Songs that Bring You to the Heart of Christmas

thegoodbook
COMPANY

Christmas Playlist
Four Songs that Bring You to the Heart of Christmas
© Alistair Begg, 2016

Published by
The Good Book Company
Tel (North America): (1) 866 244 2165
Tel (UK): 0333 123 0880
International: +44 (0) 208 942 0880
Email (North America): info@thegoodbook.com
Email (UK): info@thegoodbook.co.uk

Websites
North America: www.thegoodbook.com
UK & Europe: www.thegoodbook.co.uk
Australia: www.thegoodbook.com.au
New Zealand: www.thegoodbook.co.nz

Published in association with the literary agency of Wolgemuth and Associates, Inc.

ISBN: 9781784981662

Printed in India

Design by André Parker

Contents

Foreword

by Webb Simpson
Winner of US Open 2012

When I was young, as Christmas came along all I thought about was what gifts I might get. As I got older, I dreamed of receiving things that couldn't go under the Christmas tree. As I realized that I was good at golf, winning the US Open became the greatest gift the game could give me.

And, in 2012, it did.

But nothing that can go under the Christmas tree, and nothing that I can achieve in golf, is as good as the gift that this book is about. These things, including a US Open victory, are temporary. This book is about eternity. These things—in fact, anything that you can ever think of or want—are far exceeded by the offer Alistair focuses us on.

That's because Alistair takes us to the first Christmas and to what, or who, that first Christmas was truly all about—Jesus. In him, I've found a sense of fulfillment and peace that no number of major golf championships could ever bring me. Knowing him means I can celebrate success better and I can go through defeat better, because I can hold both in their proper place. I know they're not ultimate. And I know what is.

On the 17th hole of the final round of the 2012 US Open, when I was (as it turned out) just a few shots from winning the golf tournament I'd dreamed of winning, I had a conversation with my caddie, Paul Tesori. We reminded each other that if we won that day, it would not make any difference to our sense of satisfaction, because we couldn't take the trophy with us beyond this life anyway. There was a more important contest that would matter for all eternity, and the one who was born at that first Christmas had already won it for us.

So I'm excited about this book, and I'm excited that you've picked it up to read it. It won't take you long; you can read it over a cup of coffee. But its message can change your life—because it's the message that has changed mine, and that has given me far more than golf, or anything else in this life, ever could.

Merry Christmas!

Webb Simpson

Introduction

Christmas is Coming

Nobody announces that the Christmas season has begun. They just change the music in the stores and in the mall.

All of a sudden, you realize that you're walking through the mall to the tune of something deeply profound like "Jingle Bells" or "It's Beginning to Look a Lot Like Christmas" or "Grandma got Run Over by a Reindeer." Or maybe it's something more religious, a Christmas carol like "Once In Royal David's City" or "Hark the Herald Angels Sing."

The change of music indicates that Christmas is coming. And when Christmas is coming, there is a lot to do to get ready. So the sentimental songs and the cheesy songs and the religious songs just wash over you throughout December. They are on the radio as you make gingerbread. They are on the commercials that remind you of all the presents you haven't bought yet. They are on your playlist when you have friends over. And then, all of a sudden, it's Christmas Eve, as if the whole month has collapsed over you... and Christmas happens and then it's all over, and the songs in the stores and the mall go back to normal because it's January.

The other sign the Christmas season has begun is the appearance of nativity scenes in various places. In many ways I love them—they're a helpful reminder of what Christmas is all about, even if Mary always looks remarkably un-exhausted for someone who has just given birth, and the animals look surprisingly un-bothered at being kept from their feeding trough.

But at the same time I have a concern about nativity scenes—because I think there is a danger that they end up trivializing what they're picturing. They tend to sentimentalize the scene. We can just look at it and go, *Ahh, that's sweet. I like Christmas.* But there's nothing in it that arrests you. There's nothing there to deal with, that makes us think, that sets us back on our heels. There's nothing that says: *Listen.*

Not the Usual Christmas Songs

This book is about Christmas songs, and it invites you to peer at a nativity scene. But not the songs that wash over us, or a scene we can sentimentalize. This book takes us back to the four songs of the first Christmas, which were heard before, during and after the birth of the baby who lies at the heart of the real Christmas. That's the program.

We are going to be looking at the Gospel of Luke, one of the four historical accounts of Jesus in the Bible. And Luke, a doctor writing within living memory of the events he describes, punctuates the story of the birth of Jesus with a series of songs. He doesn't give us these songs, or poems, for them to wash over us, but for them to change us. This is a playlist that helps us to prepare for Christmas properly, and to celebrate Christmas joyfully.

Before we get into them, it is worth looking at the way in which Luke introduces his Gospel:

> *[1] Many have undertaken to draw up an account of the things that have been fulfilled among us, [2] just as they were handed down to us by those who from the first were eye-witnesses and servants of the word. [3] With this in mind, since I myself have carefully investigated everything*

> *from the beginning, I too decided to write an orderly*
> *account for you, most excellent Theophilus, [4] so that you*
> *may know the certainty of the things you have been*
> *taught. (Luke chapter 1, verses 1-4)*

Luke clearly wants it to be understood that he is reporting facts. He isn't coming up with some kind of mythological story to foist upon his friend, Theophilus, and all of the readers throughout history. He is introducing facts—staggering facts, but facts nevertheless. Luke introduces himself to us as a historian, as somebody who is very, very careful to do his investigation. He has made his investigations in order to provide sufficient basis for this individual, Theophilus—and others like Theophilus—to come to an absolute certainty regarding who Jesus is, why Jesus has come, what he has done and why it all actually matters.

Luke offers these events to us not as poetical speculation, but as pure history. That will raise the stakes for you as you read this book. Considering these events will take more thought than subconsciously humming "Jingle Bells" or idly glancing at a nativity scene—but it will be far more rewarding too. It will prove challenging and liberating, for we are considering not a sweet baby who never says anything, but the one of whom it was claimed that he was the Son of God.

I love the story of an archbishop talking to Jane Fonda, the actress. At some point the archbishop says, "Jane, Jesus is the Son of God." And she says, "Well, he may be the Son of God for you, but he isn't the Son of God for me." To which the archbishop replies, "Jane, either he is, or he isn't."

Either he is, or he isn't. My aim in this short book is to show you that he is, and why that is wonderful news for you.

1. Mary's Song
What is God Like?

What do you think about when you think about God? Which words come into your mind?

All of us have some view of God. Perhaps you think he is non-existent, or distant, or everywhere, or loving or angry or fluffy or faithful. Perhaps that view is based on an internal hunch or feeling, or on what your family believed, or on what a book or one sage or another says.

Some people expend great mental energy wrestling with the question of the reality and nature of God. Others of us give it no more than a passing thought. Whichever category we're in, everyone thinks something about God—and lots of us think different things about him.

So the question is: How do we know that we've got it right?

Imagine if you had an experience, an encounter, that enabled everything to click into place, so that you weren't just guessing, but really, truly did know about God: whether he is there and what he is like. It would be phenomenal. And it's exactly that kind of experience which kicks off most nativity plays, and which sparks the first song in Luke's account of the first Christmas— a song which gives us two words that describe the God who is really there.

This is Mary's song—a song inspired by her role in the events of the first Christmas, but in which she doesn't sing about herself, but about God. It's a song that pours out from a heart bursting with emotion.

Extraordinary Meets Ordinary

The story behind the song is familiar. The angel Gabriel has made his famous visit to Nazareth to speak to this young girl. So the background is a combination of the natural and the supernatural, the interweaving of the very ordinary and the clearly extraordinary. A lady is going to have a baby. That is ordinary news. The baby is going to be conceived by God himself. That is extraordinary news. The announcement is made by an angel sent from heaven. That is supernatural. But then Mary responds in a very natural way: *I need to go and talk to someone about this.* And so Mary "got ready and hurried to a town in the hill country of Judea," where she goes to the home of Zechariah and her relative, Elizabeth (Luke 1 v 39-40). Elizabeth is decades older, and she is pregnant too. And so now we have a kind of girl's night in. Today they would have watched a movie and had popcorn and felt each other's tummies and talked about it and said, *What are you going to do about getting a crib?* and all that kind of stuff.

And it is while Mary is with Elizabeth that she breaks out in song, the first Christmas song in history:

> *⁴⁶My soul glorifies the Lord*
> *⁴⁷and my spirit rejoices in God my Savior,*
> *⁴⁸for he has been mindful*
>   *of the humble state of his servant.*
> *From now on all generations will call me blessed,*
> *⁴⁹for the Mighty One has done great things for me—*
>   *holy is his name.*
> *⁵⁰His mercy extends to those who fear him,*
>   *from generation to generation.*
> *⁵¹He has performed mighty deeds with his arm;*
>   *he has scattered those who are proud in their*
>   *inmost thoughts.*

52He has brought down rulers from their thrones
     but has lifted up the humble.
53He has filled the hungry with good things
     but has sent the rich away empty.
54He has helped his servant Israel,
     remembering to be merciful
55to Abraham and his descendants forever,
     just as he promised our ancestors. (Luke 1 v 46-55)

Mindful of Me

Notice that Mary speaks initially in terms which are personal: "For he [that is, God] has been mindful of the humble state of his servant" (v 48). In other words, *God has been mindful of me*, Mary says. *God could have found a rich, noble, powerful queen who lived in a palace. But he has chosen not to do so. He's come instead to a lowly girl who has no apparent significance whatsoever. He's come to me.*

The Oxford English Dictionary defines "mindful" as: taking thought or taking care or keeping remembrance of something. *And*, Mary says, *this is why my soul glorifies—focuses on the greatness of—the Lord, and why my spirit rejoices in God my Savior—because he has taken thought of me. He has taken care of me. I am in his remembrance. I may be very little in the eyes of the world, but I am valuable in the eyes of the One who made the world.*

Mindful of Us

But Mary doesn't sing simply in personal terms. At the end of her song, she also sings in "people" terms: "He has helped his servant, Israel [a whole nation], remembering [that's the same word as for mindful] to be merciful to Abraham and his descendants forever, just as he promised our ancestors."

Now the significance in this is huge. God is mindful of Mary as an individual because he is mindful of his people as a whole. Her significance lies in the fact that she is part of God's plan for his people.

This is where a little history helps. Around 2,000 years before Mary sang, the God about whom she sang had made great promises to a man named Abraham. Back in the first book of the Bible, in Genesis chapter 12, he called Abraham out from his people and from his country and his household, telling him to go to a place that he would show him. And here is the promise of God to Abraham:

> *²I will make you into a great nation, and I will bless you; I will make your name great, and you will be a blessing. ³I will bless those who bless you, and whoever curses you, I will curse; and all peoples on earth will be blessed through you. (Genesis 12 v 2-3)*

All the way through the Old Testament, God says again and again to Abraham's descendants (who came to be called "Israel" and known as Jews): *I am mindful of you, I am remembering you, and I will fulfill the promise that I have made.*

He sent prophets, his spokespeople, to reaffirm the promises. So, for instance, Isaiah said six centuries before Mary was born in Israel:

> *⁶For to us a child is born, to us a son is given, and the government will be on his shoulders. And he will be called Wonderful Counsellor, Mighty God, Everlasting Father, Prince of Peace. ⁷Of the greatness of his government and peace there will be no end. He will reign on David's throne and over his kingdom, establishing and upholding it with justice and righteousness from that time on and for ever. (Isaiah 9 v 6-7)*

And the bright people of the time would have sat around and said, *Well this must be all part and parcel of the fulfilling of God's promise to Abraham. A son will be given who will fulfill all God's promises, because God is still mindful of us.*

The Son Has Been Given

And then this young woman, Mary, says that God has indeed been mindful of her, and that by being mindful of her, he has been mindful of his people as a whole. The son has been given. The promises are about to be fulfilled.

This is what God is like. He is mindful. He is personally involved with humanity. He has promised to make blessing—fulfillment and security—available to "all peoples on earth." The greatness of God is not revealed in his isolation from us; the greatness of God is revealed in his intimacy with us.

We tend to think of greatness in terms of isolation. So the more money you get, the longer you can make your driveway. Then you can get security fences, and guards. The more status you acquire, the more you can remove yourself from the great ordinary mass of humanity. People will have to come and approach you through official channels, and so on.

As a Scotsman, I'm a subject of Queen Elizabeth II. But I haven't ever had a phone call or a visit from her. She doesn't know my name. Her greatness is revealed in how isolated she is from me. But God's greatness is revealed in his intimacy with us. He does know my name, and he does know yours. He knows about, and he cares about, the responsibilities that weigh heavy on you, the quiet disappointments that gnaw at you, and the concerns that keep you awake at night. He knows about your hopes and aspirations and the moments that make your heart sing. The Creator is mindful of you, and that gives you value, whatever the world sees when it looks at you, and however you are treated by those around you. He is mindful.

All of us, whatever our background or beliefs, have a picture of God. Many of us have a God who we do not believe in because we do not like him. If you do not believe in God because he is distant, uncaring, and unhelpful, I understand. I do not believe in that God either!

Here is the God of Christmas, of history. He is a God who knows you, and he cares about you, and he makes promises to you, and he acts to help you. He is the mindful God.

Mighty Over Us

Secondly, Mary sings, *God is mighty*: "The Mighty One has done great things for me ... he has performed mighty deeds with his arm" (v 49, 51). The picture of God here is of a warrior, extending his sword-arm in strength to achieve his purposes. And what does this mighty warrior do? He turns human attitudes upside down. Notice what has he done in his might. He has taken what society, culture, and individual men and women tend to lay greatest store by—and he has demolished it.

So first, he "has scattered those who are proud in their inmost thoughts" (v 51). God does not often allow us to remain on our perch for long, if we think it is our abilities or hard work alone that put us or keeps us there. Some of the struggles that we have lived through in our lives which we tried to explain socially or economically or politically, or put down to "bad luck," should actually be explained in terms of God's mighty deeds.

Second, God has "brought down the rulers from their thrones" (v 52). Go through the whole of history and you can see that happening again and again. The proudest empires of the world eventually crumble to nothing.

And third, God sends the rich away empty even as he fills up the hungry with good things. Who are the people who shouldn't be empty? Rich people. If you are rich, you can buy what you want, eat where you like, go where you choose. Yet it is still possible to be rich and empty, not in your stomach but in your soul; because the more the rich have of the wealth that the rest of us so often prize, the emptier and more hollow things will be seen to be.

Maybe you are reading this and you know you're wealthy, but you also feel strangely empty. Maybe you are chasing more wealth, but each time you succeed, it just doesn't seem enough to fulfill you. The cliché that money cannot buy happiness is a cliché because it is true! And so is the saying, "You can't take it with you." Money cannot buy happiness and it cannot buy a way through death.

At first glance, scattering the self-reliant and sending the rich away empty seems at odds with the idea of a mindful God who cares about people. In fact, it is because God cares that he uses his might in this way. He doesn't do it vindictively. He does it purposefully. He sets people down—he removes good gifts from people—so that they might be delivered from their self-sufficient schemes and from their proud assumptions. When life is good, and successful, and comfortable, it is easy to think that we no longer need God—that we can in fact buy all we need. It is tragically easy to forget that our bodies cannot last forever, and that beyond our death we will meet with the One who is eternal. When life is good, it is easy to kid ourselves that we are mightier than we truly are, and to forget the God who is truly mightier than we are.

That's why the mighty God "has scattered those who are proud" now—to help them deal with him now, in this life. And perhaps you can see how he's done that, or is doing that, in your own life. How will you react? God wants you to see that he is not a God who fits in with all your preferences and priorities—and that's great news! He is much bigger, more mighty, and more real than that. He scatters the proud so that they can become humble. And then he lifts them up. He helps those who are humble enough to say, *I don't actually have it all together. I don't have all my questions answered. I have struggles I need help with.* God fills "the hungry with good things"—once you've realized that you're hungry for something that this world cannot give you, you're ready to find the fullness God offers.

So, what do you think about when you think about God? Mary might well have answered that question, *God is mindful of us, and more mighty than us.* And the truth that God is both all-caring and all-powerful made her heart "rejoice"—and it's a truth that causes hearts to rejoice still today.

2. Zechariah's Song
Why do You Need God?

Song lyrics seem to have a way of embedding themselves in our memory, so that as soon as we hear the first line, we know the song. Growing up in the sixties, my memorable first lines include:

"When I get older, losing my hair…"
"Hello darkness, my old friend…"
"Hey mister, that's me up on the jukebox…"
"There is a house in New Orleans…"

How did you score on knowing the songs? (If you're young enough to be struggling with these classics, google the first line to give you the song.)

When it comes to first lines, the opening words of

the song of Zechariah deserve to be in anyone's list of memorable ones. While Mary's is the first song recorded in Luke's Gospel, hers was not the first miraculous pregnancy to be described in Luke's Gospel. That belonged to her relative Elizabeth. She and her husband, Zechariah, had been "childless because Elizabeth was not able to conceive, and they were both very old" (Luke 1 v 7). But before the angel Gabriel visited Mary, he had visited Zechariah to announce that his wife would fall pregnant, and that their son, John, would grow up "to make ready a people prepared for the Lord" (v 17). John would be the warm-up act for the main event.

And that's what Zechariah sang about as his son lay in his arms. It's a song whose first line contains two words that lie at the heart of the Christmas message:

> *68Praise be to the Lord, the God of Israel,*
>   *because he has come to his people and redeemed them.*
> *69He has raised up a horn of salvation for us*
>   *in the house of his servant David*
> *70(as he said through his holy prophets of long ago),*
> *71salvation from our enemies*
>   *and from the hand of all who hate us—*
> *72to show mercy to our ancestors*
>   *and to remember his holy covenant,*

[73]the oath he swore to our father Abraham:
[74]to rescue us from the hand of our enemies,
  and to enable us to serve him without fear
[75]in holiness and righteousness before him all our days.
[76]And you, my child, will be called a prophet of the
  Most High;
  for you will go on before the Lord to prepare the way
  for him,
[77]to give his people the knowledge of salvation
  through the forgiveness of their sins,
[78]because of the tender mercy of our God,
  by which the rising sun will come to us from heaven
[79]to shine on those living in darkness
  and in the shadow of death,
  to guide our feet into the path of peace."

(Luke 1 v 68-79)

Here are the two words: "come" and "redeemed."

A Visit with a Purpose

God has come to visit. He is moving into the neighborhood. But why? To redeem. If you want to understand the first Christmas—if you want to grasp the purpose of God's visit—you need to understand redemption. So what is that about?

29

"Redemption" is the act of providing a payment to free someone. And Zechariah is explaining God's work in his present situation by referencing God's work in the past—in the time of the exodus, a millennium and a half before. It was the time when (to give an extremely cut-down summary!) God's people Israel were stuck in Egypt, enslaved by Pharaoh. Despite Pharaoh's resistance, God freed them through a series of plagues sent against the inhabitants of Egypt. The last plague was the worst—death. The oldest son in each family would die, God warned. But God also provided a way out—through the death of a lamb. The lamb died, the people who trusted God lived, and Pharaoh, devastated by what his decision to resist God had done to his nation, let them go. God had "redeemed" his people.

Well, that is great, and it is an exciting historical story—but what does it have to do with Zechariah, and what does it have to do with you and me?! Everything, actually—because, Zechariah says, God is redeeming people all over again. Not from enslavement to an Egyptian king, but from enslavement to their own sin—to our own sin. We need, he says, "forgiveness of [our] sins."

What Zechariah is referring to here is not being freed from a material plight, but a moral plight. "Sin" is an unpopular word, but it is a word the Bible una-shamedly uses, and it is a word which explains both what we see within us and what we see around us. Sin is essentially me putting myself where God deserves to be—in the place of authority and majesty, running my own life, charting my own course. It is saying to God, whether very politely or extremely angrily, *I don't want you, I won't obey your commands, I will not listen to your word. I will call the shots.*

Literally, to "sin" means to miss the mark. I don't know if you've ever seen the World Darts Champion-ships. One of the main competitions is held in England each Christmas. Two competitors stand nearly eight feet from a board 18 inches wide and throw darts at it. Thousands turn up to watch them. And the worst thing the players can do is to miss the board—to throw short or to throw wide. These contestants are wonderful at it, and it sounds very easy—but if you've never tried it, have a go. It's not as simple as it looks!

And the Bible says, "All have sinned and fall short of the glory of God" (Romans 3 v 23). Everyone throws and misses when it comes to glorifying—to recognizing, pleasing, loving and following—the God who made us, who sustains us, and who gives us everything we have. You can miss the target by an inch, or by a mile, but no one fails to miss. Often, we don't much care whether we miss or not—we are not even aiming at living in a way that pleases God, but rather one that pleases ourselves. But even when we do care and do try to obey God, we still miss. Even on my best day, I miss the mark, the target. I sin. Sin is something we choose, and yet sin is also something that traps us. We can't stop, even if we want to. Like a bad habit that proves impossible to break, we're enslaved to what we've chosen.

Spoiled and Separated

And sin is not merely a bad habit. In fact, sin is our greatest problem. People suggest that our greatest problem is a lack of education. Or a lack of social welfare. Or a lack of self-esteem. But if that's the case, then why are family gatherings at Christmas so often occasions of discord and conflict, even for the most academically gifted, well-off, personally confident people? Why is this not all fixed by now? Why is it not all sorted out? It is not fundamentally a lack of education or welfare or self-esteem that spoils things. It is sin. Sin causes alienation from others. It causes brokenness at the hands of others—and perhaps you are a victim of something that has been done to you. It causes conflict with others—not only wars on a world stage, but closer to home, conflict within our hearts, our houses, our marriages. The lies we tell. The envy we feel. The anger we show. Each time we miss the mark, we spoil our own lives and the lives of those around us.

But this "spoiled-ness" is not the most serious aspect of sin—because my sin has crippled my ability to know God and to live with God. I can't know God. I can't make my way back to God because I am trapped in my sin, enslaved by my sin. I'm stuck with being separated from God—both in my present and in my eternal future. We're cosmically stuck, hopelessly separated.

The singer, Sting, once sang:

> *"Everyone I know is lonely*
> *And God's so far away*
> *And my heart belongs to no one,*
> *So now sometimes I pray*
> *Please take the space between us*
> *And fill it up some way."*

I often hear people say that death is the great equalizer. The idea is that in eternity, all bets are off and, no matter what we believed or how we lived, the scale is reset. The Bible has a very different view. One early Christian, Paul, put it this way: "[God] has set a day when he will judge the world" (Acts 17 v 31). It will be absolutely fair and it will be completely final. There will be no redos. We have separated ourselves from God's love because we have sinned. And so we will be separated from God for all eternity, suffering the punishment of eternity in the place Jesus called "hell"—a place separated from God and everything that is good.

Actually, this view of eternity—one that includes judgment—is the one that best fits our sense of justice. Whenever we hear on the news about some terrible human act and think, *Why doesn't God do something about that?* we are asking him to judge. The Bible says that he will. All sin will be judged, and all sin will be punished by separation. That is very good news when we suffer at the hands of sinful people, and deeply troubling news because we ourselves are sinful people.

Sin is our greatest problem, because it separates us from the God whom we were made to know and designed to enjoy. But in another sense, the truth about sin is also our greatest insight, because it explains life as we experience it. There is a mighty, loving God who made us—and so we are capable of acts of greatness and kindness. But we reject that God's authority—and so we are capable of selfishness and evil. We were made to enjoy life with God eternally, but we all choose to live in defiance of him. Hence the flatness, the "blues" that come after Christmas as once again we get beyond the busyness and distraction of the festivities and think deep down, *I don't have the answer. There's not a gift I could buy or a gift I can receive that seems to satisfy. There's not a vacation I could enjoy, there's not a book I could read, or a piece of music I could listen to that will actually fill the hole.* When we feel this, we are really saying, *God, please take the space between us, and fill it up some way.* We are asking God to redeem us from the sin we have chosen—from the slavery we cannot escape and the debt we cannot repay.

Somebody's Going to Pay for This

A few years ago I was driving my brother-in-law's car round the streets of Glasgow in Scotland with my nieces in the back seat. Suddenly one of them said, "Uncle Alistair, you've gone wrong!" And while I was trying to rectify the situation, I crashed into a van. I'll never forget—this fellow jumped out immediately, and he looked at his van and he looked at me, and he said, "Somebody's going to pay for this."

That was the first (though not the only) phrase out of his mouth, and he was right. A wrong had been done. A hurt had been caused. The mark had been missed. And somebody was going to have to pay in order for things to be put right. Someone would have to bear a cost.

And someone will have to bear the cost for our sin. The mighty God who is really there does not just wink at sin. He cares about how our sin spoils the world he made, and spoils the lives of those he made. He cares about how we reject his authority and seek to sit in his place. It makes him justifiably angry. He does not just let people off. He is a God who loves justice and brings justice, and so there is a punishment to be faced—there is a price to be paid.

The problem that confronts us is that we are unable to rectify the situation. We must pay the price—unless someone comes from the outside who does not share our predicament and who can pay the price to free us from the consequences of our actions; as if my brother-in-law had turned up as that fellow in the van said, "Somebody's going to pay for this," and had dug into his wallet and paid what it would cost to restore that man's van and satisfy his justified anger. When it comes to our sin, that someone can only be God himself. We need God to come and we need God to help.

And this brings us back to Zechariah, because he is singing about the truth that God has done just that. He has turned up. And he has turned up to redeem us—to pay the price, bear the cost, of freeing us and restoring us so that we can know him and live with him again, forever.

A Question of Definition

At the heart of understanding the first Christmas, and why it is such good news, is an understanding of the nature of your predicament. And that involves accepting the nature of sinfulness—*your* sinfulness; and the seriousness of sin—*your* sin.

In other words, it involves letting God, not contemporary society, define sin. I read in a survey recently that only 17% of the American population refer to God in any way when asked to define "sin." 83% see sin as merely something negative that's had an impact on their life that they need to get cleaned up. And so they'll never understand what God was doing at the first Christmas. He did not come merely to help us put the bits and pieces of our lives together in a way that gives us wholeness and stability. He did not come to provide a little religious Energizer battery that would make us nicer people. He did not even come just to make your life happy.

He came because you were drowning, pulled down by the weight of your sin and miles from the shore. If you're drowning, it doesn't help you for someone to come along in a boat and say, *Come on now, thrash a little more. Try a little harder. Swim a bit better. You'll be able to get yourself out of that mess.* No, you need someone to reach down their hand, grasp yours, and pull you up to safety and take you to the shore. And if you know you are drowning, you don't refuse the person whose hand is offered to you. You grab it, and you splutter your gratitude.

And that is what Zechariah is doing. He knows that his son, John, will "go on before the Lord to prepare the way for him, to give his people the knowledge of salvation"—of rescue—"through the forgiveness of their sins." He knows that John will spend his life saying, *Hold on. God is coming. And God will rescue you.* And so Zechariah sings, just as everyone who grasps what God was doing at the first Christmas sings:

> *"Praise be to the Lord, the God of Israel,*
> *because he has come to his people and redeemed them."*

God was moving into the neighborhood to free people from their sins and to fill up the space between himself and sinful people—sinful you and me.

But *how* did he move in? And *how* did he fill up the space? That's what the next two songs are all about.

3. The Angels' Song
How did God Come?

Birth announcements are big business. There are so many ways to announce the entrance into the world of your little one—Pinterest, Shutterfly, WhatsApp, Tiny-Prints.com. You can take hundreds of pictures, magnify and crop them, and send them round the world. It becomes a competition. "Here's our new arrival in her crib. Here she is in her first nappy. Here she is having her first bath. Here are her footprints."

Well, if you happen to have a baby next year, here's how to outdo everyone else. Forget emails. Forget a photograph on Facebook or an entry in the *New York Times*. Here's how to win the announcement competition: *have an angel announce the birth*. Have an angel coming down the street in the middle of the night, waking your neighbors to tell them what's just happened, and then follow that up with a whole choir of angels providing celebratory backing vocals.

That's how to win. And (although sadly the angels aren't taking bookings right now) that is how the arrival of Mary's baby was announced on the night he was born:

> *8There were shepherds living out in the fields nearby, keeping watch over their flocks at night. 9An angel of the Lord appeared to them, and the glory of the Lord shone around them, and they were terrified. 10But the angel said to them, "Do not be afraid. I bring you good news that will cause great joy for all the people. 11Today in the town of David a Savior has been born to you; he is the Messiah, the Lord. 12This will be a sign to you: You will find a baby wrapped in cloths and lying in a manger."*
>
> *13Suddenly a great company of the heavenly host appeared with the angel, praising God and saying,*
> *14"Glory to God in the highest heaven,*
>   *and on earth peace to those on whom his favor rests."*
> *(Luke 2 v 8-14)*

God's Name

The angel told these shepherds who it was who had been growing in Mary's womb, and who was now "wrapped in cloths and lying in a manger." He described the baby's job—"Savior": Redeemer. He announced the baby's title—"Messiah": God's King promised for centuries to his people, promises recorded for us in the Old Testament. And he revealed the baby's identity—"the Lord."

And that word, "Lord," is making a staggering claim, because it is the word that was used by Greek-speaking Jews to translate the Hebrew word "Yahweh"—the personal name of God, by which he had introduced himself to his people for centuries. "God" is not God's name, any more than "Pastor" is mine. My name is Alistair, and my friends call me that. God's name is Yahweh, and it's what he told his friends, his people, to call him. In other words, here's the deal: good news, great joy for all the people, has come because a Redeemer, the ultimate Ruler, has been born. And he is God Almighty.

Every so often at Christmas, we hear about a wealthy businessman who's gone and served in a soup kitchen, or about a very successful athlete who spends some time on Christmas Eve in the children's hospital. And everyone says, "That's great—what an amazing and kind and humble thing for him to do." And it is. But now see what this angel is saying: *The God who made you, who gave you your DNA, who woke you up this morning, who has sustained your life—that God, in the person of Jesus, stepped down into time, making himself accessible.*

On the first Christmas night—and this is the heart of the Christmas story, and the heart of the Christian faith—God took on flesh. The voice that made the cosmos could be heard crying in the cradle. The hands that placed each star in its place grabbed hold of Mary's fingers. Her son was fully human, and fully God. In this man, divinity met humanity.

So, unlike every other conception and birth, this was not the beginning. God the Son had always existed, equal with and eternal with the Father and the Spirit—one God in three persons, what often is called the Trinity. God the Son—the "Word"—predates his birth; he is older than his conception, or what is often called his incarnation:

> *[1]In the beginning was the Word, and the Word was with God, and the Word was God. [2]He was with God in the beginning. (John 1 v 1-2)*

I remember my daughter when she was young once asking me, "Where was I before I was born?" And the answer is, "You did not exist before you were conceived and born." (I avoided mention of the conception part when I answered my daughter.) But that's not what happened with Jesus. He did exist before he was conceived and born. What happened that night was the birth of God the Son as a human. But it was not the beginning of the person God the Son.

This is unparalleled. It is unique. It is mysterious. And Luke is claiming that it is historical.

A Virgin Birth—Really?

Perhaps this is where you struggle with the Christian faith. You are prepared to accept Jesus as a great teacher, a religious leader, or a brilliant philosopher. You are prepared to accept that he spoke for God, perhaps. But you struggle to accept that he *is* God—that as Mary and Joseph peered into the manger, they were looking at the eternal Son of God. You struggle with the idea of a virgin birth and a miraculous incarnation.

Well, if your starting point is that there is no God, then the incarnation question is irrelevant. If there is no God, he could not have been born as a baby in Bethlehem. But if your starting point is that there is (or even that there might be) a God who created the entire universe, then surely he is capable of entering his universe.

Why would we be surprised that he can do what he wants to do? After all, in the last century or so humanity has worked out how to bring about conception without sexual intercourse. A hundred years ago, that idea would have seemed impossible and not worthy of being believed. Now it seems plausible and obvious. If doctors can do it in their way, do we really want to say that God cannot do it in his? God the Son taking flesh is a mystery that we will never understand. But not being able to understand how God became one of us is not proof that he did not become one of us.

Of course God's ways are mysterious and at times inexplicable to us! He would not be much of a God if our limited minds could reason out everything about him.

No, this is mystery, because it is divinity; it is God—but it is also history. Heaven is breaking into earth. The shepherds would find the Creator of the universe wrapped in strips of cloth. Here is the answer to the human predicament, the solution to our slavery to sin and our separation from God. God bridged the gap by coming from heaven to earth. This is how much the mighty God cares about us. Love was when God spanned the gulf. Love was when God became a man. Love was when God surprised those he had created by being born as one of them—as a baby.

The God of Surprises

But that is not the only surprise. The place where God's Son was born is also a surprise, and the people to whom God sent the angels is a third surprise. And they show us something of what God is like.

First, look where the God-child is. "You will find a baby wrapped in cloths and lying in a manger." It was not unusual to have a baby in swaddling cloths. It was unusual to lay a baby in a food trough.

In human terms, the reason why Mary had her child in a shack (or very possibly a cave) used for sheltering animals was straightforward. In distant Rome the emperor, Caesar Augustus, had ordered that a census be taken, obliging Mary and Joseph to travel from Nazareth to Bethlehem, and there was no room for them to stay anywhere else. Augustus meant "worthy of adoration." According to an inscription on a stone carved in around 9 BC and found in a marketplace in what is now Turkey, Augustus' birth "gave the whole world a new aspect." He was regarded as a "Savior." He encouraged the worship of his adoptive father, Julius Caesar, as a god, and allowed himself to be styled as "the son of God." So great was his power and his impact that the inscription continued that "from his birth a new reckoning of time must begin."

And so the shepherds must surely have been struck by how vastly different this child in a manger was from the power and majesty of the Roman Emperor, from this Caesar Augustus figure—from the person who established the glory of his name and the might of his empire at the head of his armies, and who could move his subject peoples around at the stroke of a pen. And yet here in this food trough lay the one who really is worthy of adoration, whose birth changes everything, who came as Savior and who really is the Son of God—and whose birth-date is the way we still reckon our time 2,000 years later.

He was not born to a queen, in a palace. He was born to a girl, in a cave, and his cradle was a food trough. The Son of God came to be just like us, among us, rather than to lord it over us. If you have known poverty, so has he. If you have known what it feels like to be an outsider, so has he. His was not a gilded, protected existence. He knows what life is like. As Jesus himself put it when he had grown up, he "did not come to be served, but to serve, and to give his life as a ransom for many" (Mark 10 v 45).

The second surprise is where the announcement was made. God did not make his announcement to Augustus. It came to a group of poor shepherds. We might expect that God would be most interested in those who had status, those who were powerful, those who were mighty. In actual fact, throughout Luke's Gospel, we discover that again and again he goes for the least and last and the left out. He works in a way that we might not anticipate him working. And we have to allow him to surprise us: to be different than a god we would make up, and to work differently than how we would if we were God. This is the real God, and you and I are not him. People find it perfectly easy to tolerate Jesus just to the point where he contravenes their expectations—and then they tend to have a very different response.

Peace Offer

So that's the message of the angel—but no sooner have the shepherds picked themselves up off the ground than the reinforcements appear. The Redeemer has come and the angels of heaven are there to announce it for him.

And the choir declares what this baby will achieve: "On earth peace." Augustus had established what was known as the "Pax Romana"—an empire at peace and guaranteeing safety (unless you happened to be a slave or a rebel). But the peace of Rome was about to be dwarfed by the peace of God. Epictetus, a first-century philosopher, observed rightly that:

> "*While the emperor may give peace from war on land and sea, he is unable to give peace from passion, grief and envy; he cannot give peace of heart, for which man yearns for more than even outward peace.*"

Caesar Augustus could not transform any of his subjects' hearts or change any of their eternal futures.

But, the angels say, this baby could. Here is an announcement of a peace that goes deep within, and lasts beyond the grave—the peace "for which man yearns." The peace *of* God that invades a life is based on the discovery of peace *with* God.

Today, our newspapers are filled with all kinds of attempts at peace. Peace between husbands and wives, between family members, between nations, and so on. But Epictetus is still right—peace of heart proves elusive. No matter how well we do at trying to establish peace with each other, until we discover what it is to have peace with God, we're not going to discover the peace of God.

And, since we are separated from God—since we have declared independence and rebelled against our rightful Ruler—this is a peace that can only be brought about by the intervention of God himself. We may try to find peace without God in our own way—peace through owning stuff; peace at the bottom of a bottle. We may try to find peace with God in our own strength—peace through obeying religious rules or through being "good people." But the truth is that only God can give us peace with himself. The angels tell us where his offer of peace was made. This is a peace that isn't found in something. It's a peace that is found in someone. And it is a peace that pursues us, seeks us, comes knocking on the door of our lives.

But it's a peace that so many miss out on because they fail to make room for the one who brings it. Remember why Jesus was lying in a manger in the first place? Why was the God of heaven in a feeding trough? Because there was no room anywhere else. No one had made room for him. He made the entire universe. He came into his universe. And there wasn't a place for him.

Let's be honest; in the lives of many of us, it's no different. We have no room for him either—not if it makes life in any way uncomfortable for us, not if his presence brings any inconvenience to us, not when his actions and words surprise us. But our response does not change the truth. God has visited this world. He has come as one of us, to bring peace to us by redeeming us from our sins. Will you say to him, "No room?"

4. Simeon's Song
How did God do it?

Of all the things that are said when someone takes a little baby into their arms, many are quite silly and said out of embarrassment. We don't know what to say and so we just come out with, "My, he has his mother's nose" or, "Can you believe how much hair he has?" or whatever else. Older men are often the worst at knowing what to say in this situation (I know, because I am one of them).

But our fourth and final "singer" was in no doubt about what he would say when he held the infant Jesus in his arms the first time Jesus was brought to Jerusalem, the capital, and to the temple, the center of Jewish religious life. His name was Simeon. He was a devout believer in God. He was patiently waiting for the promises God had made to be fulfilled. And not only that, but God's Holy Spirit had told him that he wouldn't die until he saw these promises begin to unfold on the pages of history.

> ^{27}*When the parents brought in the child Jesus …*
> ^{28}*Simeon took him in his arms and praised God, saying:*
> ^{29}*"Sovereign Lord, as you have promised,*
> * you may now dismiss your servant in peace.*
> ^{30}*For my eyes have seen your salvation,*
> ^{31}*which you have prepared in the sight of all nations:*
> ^{32}*a light for revelation to the Gentiles,*
> * and the glory of your people Israel." (Luke 2 v 27-32)*

The angels had brought the news that a Savior had been born. Likewise, Simeon announces the truth that he is looking at God's salvation, lying in his arms. And Simeon understands that this Savior has come to save not only "your people Israel"—the ancient people of God, the descendants of Abraham—but he has also come "to the Gentiles"—everyone else. If you carry on reading Luke's Gospel, you find the adult Jesus living this out. People think he's going to go for the religious folks, and he doesn't—he hangs out with the irreligious folks. People think he's going to go for the people who are doing their best, but he doesn't—he welcomes the people who have done worst. That's because he has come to bring to light and then deal with their greatest problem, whether they are religious or irreligious, good or bad—their sin. As the angels promised, this child would be good news of great joy for all people. There is no one who does not need Jesus to offer them salvation, and no one to whom he does not offer that salvation.

So this old man is now content to die. He has been waiting his whole life for this one sight, and now he has seen it—the Sovereign Lord's salvation, in the shape of a human, lying in his arms.

Your Heart will Break

But Simeon did not only speak of salvation. He spoke of suffering too. He had more to say to Mary:

> [34]*This child is destined to cause the falling and rising of many in Israel, and to be a sign that will be spoken against,* [35]*so that the thoughts of many hearts will be revealed. And a sword will pierce your own soul too.*
>
> *(v 34-35)*

He was explaining, or rather hinting at, what was to come—not just announcing that this child would bring salvation, but hinting at what it would cost him to bring it. He was the child who would cause many to fall, and others to rise. He would reveal the deep secrets, and the true attitude towards God, that lies in every human heart. He would be opposed verbally; and one day, his mother's soul would be torn apart emotionally. Imagine taking a newborn child in your arms, then looking at his mom and saying, *One day, your heart will break because of this child.* That is what Simeon is warning of here. He does not tell Mary what will happen; but he does tell Mary how it will feel.

Easter at Christmas

My guess is that Mary never forgot Simeon's words, nor that she really understood them, until the other end of her child's life. As an adult, the one who had lain in the devout Simeon's cradling arms was hung from a cruel Roman cross. But this is Easter—and isn't this a book about Christmas?! Yes, but unless you understand the events of Easter, you'll never grasp the heart of Christmas. Simeon understood that—which is why he pointed forwards to Good Friday even as he welcomed the baby at the center of Christmas. Simeon is pointing us to how God redeemed his people.

So let's move forward three decades or so, from near

the beginning to almost the end of Luke's Gospel. Let us see what Mary saw, which Simeon had warned her of:

> [32]*Two other men, both criminals, were also led out with him to be executed.* [33]*When they came to the place called the Skull, they crucified him there, along with the criminals—one on his right, the other on his left.* [34]*Jesus said, "Father, forgive them, for they do not know what they are doing." And they divided up his clothes by casting lots.* [35]*The people stood watching, and the rulers even sneered at him. They said, "He saved others; let him save himself if he is God's Messiah, the Chosen One."*
>
> [36]*The soldiers also came up and mocked him. They offered him wine vinegar* [37]*and said, "If you are the king of the Jews, save yourself."*
>
> [38]*There was a written notice above him, which read:* THIS IS THE KING OF THE JEWS.
>
> [39]*One of the criminals who hung there hurled insults at him: "Aren't you the Messiah? Save yourself and us!"*
> [40]*But the other criminal rebuked him. "Don't you fear God," he said, "since you are under the same sentence?* [41]*We are punished justly, for we are getting what our deeds deserve. But this man has done nothing wrong."*
> [42]*Then he said, "Jesus, remember me when you come into your kingdom."*

> *⁴³Jesus answered him, "Truly I tell you, today you will be with me in paradise."*
> *⁴⁴It was now about noon, and darkness came over the whole land until three in the afternoon, ⁴⁵for the sun stopped shining. And the curtain of the temple was torn in two. ⁴⁶Jesus called out with a loud voice, "Father, into your hands I commit my spirit." When he had said this, he breathed his last.*
> *⁴⁷The centurion, seeing what had happened, praised God and said, "Surely this was a righteous man."*
>
> *(Luke 23 v 32-47)*

It's easy to miss the strange fact that there are virtually no details here of Jesus' physical suffering. Luke wants you to look at this scene, but he does not want you to focus on the outward aspects, the physical horror of it, and so overlook the deeper emotional and spiritual aspects of what is going on (the aspects that Simeon had not overlooked in his words to Jesus' mother). Luke doesn't want you to feel only sympathy for Jesus as a sufferer—because he wants you to put your faith in Jesus as your Savior. He wants you and me to grasp not only what Jesus suffered, but how he saves. Luke is painting a picture; and as we stand back and look at the scene, I think there are three things that stand out for us.

Dispute over the Clothes

First, the dispute over the clothes. As Jesus died, the soldiers divided up Jesus' clothes by casting lots. Jewish men tended to wear five garments, and soldiers at an execution were allowed to keep the condemned man's clothes. Perhaps they divided four of the items among themselves:

> *I want the sandals—you got the sandals from the last guy. It's your turn for the turban.*
> *I don't want the turban. But alright, I'll take it.*
> *OK, but what are we going to do with this undergarment? It's just one huge piece.*
> *Well, why don't we throw dice for it?*

When you go into the hospital, they take your clothes from you and give you one of those gowns that you struggle to tie at the back. I think it's to let you know that you are now in their control. You're completely in their hands. You give your clothes away, and you hope you'll be able to get them back on the other side of your procedure. If someone else gets them back, it means that things did not go according to plan.

Jesus is not going to get his clothes back. The point here is that he is left with nothing; he is reduced to nothing. This man's birth had been announced by angels.

In between his birth and death, he had commanded storms, multiplied meals for one into banquets for thousands, re-started a dead girl's life, stood up to those who used religion as a veneer for their own desires for power or wealth, and offered compassion to those broken in their bodies or by their mistakes. Now Jesus is nothing, and has nothing. Even a criminal condemned to death and hanging alongside him speaks against him (just as Simeon had foretold). He looks at Jesus and says, in effect:

> *I'm not sure what the Messiah, God's great Ruler, is supposed to be like, but I'm pretty certain that he shouldn't be hanging on a cross. If you really were who you claim to be, you'd save yourself. You'd get yourself off the cross. And you'd get us off too. But you're not doing that—you fake.*

Jesus is plumbing the depths. Naked, vulnerable, and mocked by a dying criminal.

Why?

Darkness During the Day

To understand, we need to look at the second detail that stands out: darkness during the day. In the Bible, darkness during the day is a signal of God's displeasure and God's judgment. Remember that it was Israel's rescue from

Egypt—the exodus—that helped explain what "redemption" is? Well, it is that rescue that also explains what the darkness means. The last plague was the judgment of God, and it came to everyone in Egypt—whether Egyptian or a member of Israel—because everyone had sinned. So in each house, the firstborn son died, unless a lamb had died in that home. But the second-last plague was the plague of darkness. "Total darkness covered all Egypt for three days" (Exodus 10 v 22). That darkness was an indication of impending judgment. That darkness said to everyone in Egypt that God's punishment was falling—that the punishment of death and separation from him, the punishment deserved by sinners who have lived in rejection of him, was coming.

But as darkness fell over Israel on the afternoon that Jesus was nailed to the cross, only one man "breathed his last"—Jesus. God's judgment had come—and it was God, in the person of his Son, who was experiencing it. On the cross, Jesus entered into a realm he'd never experienced. Here we have God, abandoned by God. Here we see God's Son, punished as a sinner by his Father, even though he had never, ever sinned—never failed to love his Father and his neighbor. Jesus was experiencing the real abandonment of his Father. He was experiencing hell.

Why? Because Jesus was bearing the burden of the world's sin. Jesus was not dying as the firstborn, since he had never sinned. He was dying as the lamb. He was paying the price to redeem people. He was going through hell so that he could save people from hell—in those agonising hours, he was losing friendship with his Father so others could gain it.

It is what some people call the great exchange. God the Son took on the penalty due to sinful people, and so God the Father declares guilty sinners who trust Jesus as forgiven, guilt-free. I deserve to be on the cross; Jesus hung on it. My sin deserved punishment; Jesus took it.

How do we know this is what he did? Because of the third detail from the scene that we need to focus on.

Divine Vandalism in the Temple

As Jesus died on the cross, an act of divine vandalism took place only yards from where he had once lain in Simeon's arms. "The curtain of the temple was torn in two." There were two massive curtains in the temple, about eighty feet high, and both were huge visual reminders of the truth that there is a separation between sinful man and the perfect God. We're not talking about some flimsy curtain here—we're talking about a curtain that defines what it means to be a curtain. It would be impossible for even the strongest human to tear it. I mean, have you ever tried to open one of those bags of airline peanuts?! There's no way that a species that struggles with that can tear in two an 80-foot high curtain.

So who tore it? God tore it. *God* tore it? Tore his own curtain? Vandalized his own temple? Filled up the space between us and him? Punished his own Son? Opened the way to him so that we need not be stuck with our sin and separated from him? Threw open the door of heaven? *Yes.* That's why the Father sent his Son, and why his Son went to the cross. The cross shows me that my sin is very real and is absolutely horrendous—it took the death of God's only Son to deal with it and free me from it. But the cross also shows me that God is very real and awesomely loving—God the Son came to die so that my sin could be dealt with.

And this is why the wooden food trough led to the wooden cross, and why you will never get to the heart of Christmas if you don't grasp the meaning of Easter. Christianity is not good advice about what we should do. It is the good news of what Christ has done. Christianity does not proclaim that you are worth saving or able to save yourself. It announces that God is mighty to save.

Paid

Do you like paying bills? I actually love it—I think it is because of the satisfaction and relief of getting it dealt with. I don't like that I have to pay the bill—but I do like getting the bill paid. And it is especially satisfying to pay a bill in person. You walk over to the counter and you pay for it, and then you have the joy of seeing someone take your bill and write PAID. I prefer it actually when it is a stamp that stamps PAID in red with double circles.

As long as I have that bill marked PAID, no one can make me pay again. It's been settled. It is all over, paid for, in the past.

And three days after the events that must have pierced Mary's soul, God stamped PAID unmistakably against all the sins I have committed, all the debt I owe to him. After all, the death of Jesus could have been merely a tragic incident. The afternoon darkness and the ripped-apart curtain could have been sheer coincidences. Within hours, his corpse lay cold in a tomb. But three days later, God the Father left no one in any doubt that he had accepted Jesus' payment for sinners' debts—that the price to free sinners had been paid:

> *[1]On the first day of the week, very early in the morning, the women took the spices they had prepared and*

went to the tomb. ²They found the stone rolled away from the tomb, ³but when they entered, they did not find the body of the Lord Jesus. ⁴While they were wondering about this, suddenly two men in clothes that gleamed like lightning stood beside them. ⁵In their fright the women bowed down with their faces to the ground, but the men said to them, "Why do you look for the living among the dead? ⁶He is not here; he has risen! Remember how he told you, while he was still with you in Galilee: ⁷'The Son of Man must be delivered over to the hands of sinners, be crucified and on the third day be raised again.'"

(Luke 24 v 1-7)

Luke's Gospel finishes in a very similar place to where it began. We began with angels appearing, and we finish the same way. We began with an angel announcing the presence of life where it is, humanly-speaking, impossible—in the wombs of a woman who was infertile and a woman who was a virgin. We finish with angels announcing the presence of life in a tomb—the resurrection of a crucified criminal to eternal glory.

And between the events of the first Christmas Eve and the first Easter Sunday, Simeon's words had come true. Jesus had reached out to those who were outsiders, excluded. He had been opposed. He had revealed what people really believed. Physical nails had pierced his hands as an emotional sword pierced the soul of his watching mother. And, as he hung on the cross, he had redeemed his people—he died the death that tore the curtain and he paid the price that bought the salvation that Simeon had spoken of all those years before.

He died on that cross because Simeon, Mary, Zechariah, the shepherds, you and I are sinners—and because he loves them, and us, anyway.

Conclusion

Once in Royal David's City...

Most of us have a favorite carol. Mine is "Once in Royal David's City." I wish they would play it in our local mall—because it takes us to the heart of Christmas. In a sense, I could have just printed the words for you to read, instead of making you read four chapters in this book. It's too late for that now, but it's not too late to think about it briefly in this conclusion.

Here are four reasons why I love this carol. First, it begins with history:

"Once in royal David's city."

That means the events it describes happened in a time-frame. And they happened in a geographical location—

the city where the greatest Old Testament king of Israel, David, grew up: Bethlehem. There was a point in history when this event actually occurred, in a real place and at a real time. Luke and the other Gospel writers did not set out to write stories—they set out to record history. Have you understood that the Gospels are not fables—that they are facts?

Second, this carol takes us unashamedly to divinity:

"He came down to earth from heaven."

The second person of the Trinity—the eternal, Creator God—came from heaven and stepped into time and lived in his creation. The baby born in Bethlehem that first Christmas night was God—God moving into the neighborhood.

If Jesus were just a remarkable man, or a prophet, or a great teacher, then we will stumble here. If that's who we've determined he was, then we will have issues with the virgin birth. We will struggle with the idea of miracles. We will be unable to believe in the resurrection. But once we acknowledge that the baby born in Bethlehem was God, then that makes sense of everything we read in the Gospels. Suddenly, this man walking on water, turning water into wine and feeding five thousand with a boy's lunch is not only possible, it's what we'd expect to see, because the Creator has shown up. When we read the Gospels, we read what happened when divinity entered history.

And, as we've seen, he entered history as a human. Christmas is a story of humanity:

"He was little, weak and helpless,
Tears and smiles like us he knew."

This line is often dismissed as Victorian sentimentality. It's not. Babies are helpless. In fact, adults often are too. Babies are moved to cry and to giggle. Adults often are too. God came to earth as a helpless human baby—that is amazing. And he lived on earth as a real man, experiencing the ups and downs that are part of our lives—that is wonderful.

History, divinity, humanity—and lastly, majesty:

"And he leads his children on
To the place where he has gone.
Not in that poor lowly stable,
With the oxen standing by,
We shall see him, but in heaven,
Set at God's right hand on high."

God became a man so that man could live with God. The baby Jesus grew into the man who died on a cross so that he could open the way to heaven. He became the man who rose from the tomb so that he could rule from heaven, at his Father's right hand. And he became the man who sent his Spirit to open people's eyes to the truth about him. We shall all see him at God's right hand on high. We all have an appointment with him there.

On Thin Ice

And that is why the first Christmas draws a dividing line. Mary, remember, spoke of God's work of scattering "those who are proud in their inmost thoughts" even as he "lifted up the humble." Simeon, we saw in the last chapter, warned that her child would be the cause of people falling as well as rising. Christmas provokes a decision. At the first Christmas, Jesus came to you. Now you must decide: will you come to him?

I'm not talking about you becoming a religious person, or a more religious person. I'm not talking about you adding a little spirituality to your life. I'm not talking about you trying harder to be good, or to do things that God would like. The dividing line is not between those who go along to church and those who do not, or those who are committed to attending Bible classes and those who are not. It is not between the good and the bad.

The dividing line is between those who have placed

their faith in Jesus, and those who have placed it in something or someone else.

We have a pond in our neighborhood. A couple of Christmases ago, I walked past it with a friend.

"Maybe I'll go skate on that pond," he said.

"I don't think you should," I replied.

"I'm sure it'll be fine," he argued.

"I don't care how sure you are," I said. "You weigh 170 pounds and the pond is only frozen to 3/8 of an inch. It cannot possibly support you. You would be crazy to put your weight on it."

He decided not to go skating.

My friend had faith in the ice. But his faith would not have saved him—in fact, his faith could have drowned him. Why? Because the object of his faith could not support him.

If the ice had been thicker, my response would have been very different. If the pond was frozen to a depth of three feet, then he and I could both have gone skating.

It is not the amount of faith that matters. It is the foundation of the faith that counts. And the message of Christmas is that the baby who was born can bear the weight of your life and your eternity. He came to be your Ruler—in charge of every part of your life, showing you how to live the life that you were created to live, that pleases him and satisfies you. He came to be your Redeemer—to die for you so that you can live forever with him.

We all have faith. We all trust someone or something to help us through life, to tell us how to make decisions with our life, and then to lead us through death. It might be yourself. It might be someone else. It might be a theory or a philosophy or a religion. But all these are thin ice. They will crack, either in this life or when you reach your death. The heart of the first Christmas is that God was giving you himself, so that you might accept him as your Ruler and rely on him as your Redeemer—so that you might place your faith in him and enjoy a faith that saves you.

This is the central and crucial difference between religion and Christianity.

Religion says, *Clean up your act and maybe God will accept you.*
Christianity says, *God accepts you because of who Jesus is and because of what he's done.*

Religion says, *Do this, live this way, and you'll be accepted.*
Christianity says, *Through faith in Jesus, you are accepted; now live this way, do this.*

So a Christian is someone who treats Jesus as their Ruler, in charge of their life; and trusts him as their

Redeemer, able to bring them through death. It is some-one who recognizes whom God was giving us at the first Christmas, and that this is the greatest gift of any Christmas.

Open the Gift

So it is up to you. God has offered you a Son-shaped gift. Now that gift has to be received.

A couple of Decembers ago, I was sitting next to our Christmas tree the day after Christmas. And I looked down, and there was a small box sitting under the tree, just by my hand. And I picked it up and turned it over, and it had a label on it, and the label said, *For Alistair.*

"Oh," I said to no one in particular. "There's a present I haven't opened."

I knew what it was by looking at it and shaking it. It was golf balls—which is a much-needed gift for a man of my (in)ability on the fairways (and surrounding areas). I knew what was in it. But I still needed to open it, so that I could use it and enjoy it.

The Bible says that "the wages of sin is death, but the gift of God is eternal life in Christ Jesus our Lord" (Romans 6 v 23). Perhaps you've left that gift under the tree year by year. Perhaps you've never noticed it before. Perhaps you've seen it, but ignored it. Perhaps you've never realized what it was, or never realized it was for you, or never realized how much you needed it.

I hope this book has shown you that the gift on offer to you is redemption through faith in Jesus, the Son of God... that it is for you... and that you desperately need it. And I hope that, this Christmas, you will not leave under the tree that unopened gift with your name on it—especially as it comes from God.

....

Perhaps you have reached a point where you have realized you need to take the claims of Jesus seriously, and to think hard about what was really going on at the first Christmas. If you want to, you can get in touch with me via info@thegoodbook.com, and I will try to link you up with some people local to you who would love to talk all this through with you.

But it may well be that you are ready to accept God's offer and receive his gift. If you know that this is you, then speak to him now. You could say something like:

God,

Thank you that your Son Jesus came to earth at the first Christmas. I admit that I have rejected your rule, sought to live without you, and that there is a gap between us. I am sorry for my sin.

Thank you that Jesus died to bear the burden of my sin, and to take away that separation. Thank you that Jesus rose to rule, and to offer me life forever with you.

I am accepting that gift. I want to live with Jesus as my Ruler, and I trust him as my Redeemer. I am putting my faith in him; I am placing my eternity in his hands.

Please help me to live out this decision.

If you have said and meant this, your eternity has changed! And once again, if you reach out to me at info@thegoodbook.com, then I would love to connect you to some Christians in your neighborhood, who can celebrate with you and can help you as you start out on the first few days of your new, eternal, life.

A Christmas Gift

We hope you've enjoyed looking at these songs from the first Christmas with Alistair Begg. It's our delight to offer you a very special early Christmas gift: a free Christmas song from the internationally acclaimed Keith and Kristyn Getty. Visit the site below and enter the promo code **gettyfree** to download and enjoy this Christmas music.

Merry Christmas!

The Good Book Company

thegoodbook.com/free-song

If you enjoyed
Christmas Playlist

then you'll also enjoy reading...

Based on seven episodes in Luke's Gospel, *Original Jesus* introduces the Jesus of history—the one who often gets hidden behind all the other versions of Jesus we're offered. The Jesus who is controversial, compassionate, sometimes uncomfortable, often unpredictable... and completely real.

"Reading this book is like having a conversation with a friend."
Dr Kathleen Nielson, author of Resting Secure

thegoodbook
COMPANY
Opening up the Bible

Thanks for reading this book. We hope you enjoyed it, and found it helpful.

Most people want to find answers to the big questions of life: Who are we? Why are we here? How should we live? But for many valid reasons we are often unable to find the time or the right space to think positively and carefully about them.

At The Good Book Company, we're passionate about producing materials that help people of all ages and stages understand the heart of the Christian message, which is found in the pages of the Bible.

Whoever you are, and wherever you are at when it comes to these big questions, we hope we can help. As a publisher we want to help you look at the good book that is the Bible because we're convinced that as we meet the person who stands at its centre—Jesus Christ—we find the clearest answers to our biggest questions.

Visit our website to discover the range of books, videos and other resources we produce, or visit our partner site www.christianityexplored.org for a clear explanation of who Jesus is and why he came.

Thanks again for reading,

Your friends at The Good Book Company

NORTH AMERICA
UK & EUROPE
AUSTRALIA
NEW ZEALAND

 thegoodbook.com
thegoodbook.co.uk
thegoodbook.com.au
thegoodbook.co.nz

 866 244 2165
0333 123 0880
(02) 6100 4211
(+64) 3 343 2463

 WWW.CHRISTIANITYEXPLORED.ORG
Our partner site is a great place for those exploring the Christian faith, with a clear explanation of the good news, powerful testimonies and answers to difficult questions.